Copyright © 2015   Scott Shoob

First Printing, July 22nd 2015

Beit Tefillah Publishing, All rights Reserved

No part of this book may be printed or distributed without the expressed, written consent of the author.

The Shemitah

How We Prepared For It

Scott Shoob

Foreword by Joseph F Dumond

For many years we have encouraged people to keep the Sabbatical years. Yes, we have shown you in our book *"Remembering the Sabbatical year of 2016"* how to prove beyond all doubts, using your own bible to do so, and then backing this up with many historical references.

So it is with great pleasure to see others also realizing the importance of obeying Yehovah, our Creator and taking care of the land as He has directed us in letting it rest every seventh year. We used to call this fallowing the land.

Back then when we used the word fallowing the land people also stored much of their own foods. Today most do not live on the land and they do not know how to store food or prepare their food to be stored.

If and when the stores are ever shut down for any host of reasons, those who have stored food or know how to store food will do much better than those who make a daily or weekly trip to the grocery store for their existence.

It is by taking care of the land, by letting it rest every seventh year, that we also eliminate many of the climate problems that now plague the world. These curses and plagues are a result of not obeying our Creator: Of not keeping the weekly Sabbath, the Holy Days of Leviticus 23 and these curses are a result of not letting the land rest at the proper time. The Shemitah is to be kept from the month of Aviv 2016 to the month of Aviv 2017 and then every seventh year after that.

We are commanded not to plant and we are not to harvest. We are also commanded to stock up food in the sixth year, like Israel did the manna on the sixth day, a double portion. We are also commanded to forgive debts of those who owe you, both sins and financial. We are commanded to release the Hebrew slaves we may have in our possession. We are commanded to read the Torah during the Feast of Sukkot in the Sabbatical year (Deuteronomy 31:10-13). By doing this you and your family will be blessed. By not doing so your family is missing out on the blessings Yehovah wants to give you.

This book about how to prepare food to be stored for the Shemitah year is very appropriate for those who are just learning about the Shemitah and to help them to get ready. Read it and help others to get ready to obey the laws of the Kingdom of Yehovah.

May Yehovah bless those who keep His Torah. May Yehovah bless you and reveal the deeper understandings of words to those who keep the Sabbath, the Holy Days and the Sabbatical years. May you grow closer to Yehovah by walking in His commandments and learning how His Kingdom, the world and universe work.

Shalom.

Joseph F Dumond
www.sightedmoon.com

Within this book, we are not providing any type of guide for which years comprise the seven-year Shemitah cycle. We know that the new year begins in the spring as that is based on scripture (Exodus/Shemot 12:2). A lot of Jewish tradition (and some popular authors) would have us believe that the Shemitah starts in the fall, which is based on tradition and is incorrect.

If we are going to observe YHWH's Shemitah, we should make every attempt to do it right. We must search the scriptures and learn to separate what man says from what YHWH commands, as quite often they do not match. And we must pray for YHWH's help and guidance.

One of the best authors we have found on the subject of the Shemitah/Sabbatical Years is the author of the foreword to this book, Joseph F. Dumond of sightedmoon.com. He has most probably done more research to pinpoint the correct years of the Shemitah and the Jubilee than any other in modern times. Both the observance and timing of these moedim or appointed times of the Creator were lost to us, and through his diligent research and other witnesses to his facts, we can thank YHWH we have them back!

Please consider purchasing Dumond's book for further study:

"Remembering The Sabbatical Years of 2016: Breaking The Curses By Obedience"

REMEMBERING THE SABBATICAL YEARS OF
2016
2023
2030
2037
2044

JOSEPH F. DUMOND

sightedmoon
www.sightedmoon.com

Leviticus 25:1 *And YHWH spoke to Mosheh on Mount Sinai, saying,*

Leviticus 25:2 *"Speak to the children of Israel, and say to them, 'When you come into the land which I give you, then the land shall observe a Sabbath to YHWH.*

Leviticus 25:3 *'Six years you sow your field, and six years you prune your vineyard, and gather in its fruit,*

Leviticus 25:4 *but in the seventh year the land is to have a Sabbath of rest, a Sabbath to YHWH. Do not sow your field and do not prune your vineyard.*

Leviticus 25:5 *'Do not reap what grows of its own of your harvest, and do not gather the grapes of your unpruned vine, for it is a year of rest for the land.*

Leviticus 25:6 *'And the Sabbath of the land shall be to you for food, for you and your servant, and for your female servant and your hired servant, and for the stranger who sojourns with you,*

Leviticus 25:7 *and for your livestock and the beasts that are in your land. All its crops are for food.*

The Shemitah. The Sabbath of the land.

During the Shemitah, we are told to let the land rest. And this is not only the ground that we own, that we rent, or that is in our custody, but we are told to prepare so that ALL the land can rest.

We have been kept in the dark for so long; all of this was sealed up and hidden from us as we have been lied to by modern religion who tells us "we don't do these things any more." If you are reading this book, there's a good chance you no longer believe their lies, and this is why you desire to obey YHWH and keep his Torah, his feast days and moedim, which include the Shemitah.

We realize that we are to let the land rest. Now what? What do we do to prepare for this year-long period when we cannot plant or harvest? What do we store, can, or purchase now in the preparation year so as not to violate the Shemitah? We need to make sure we understand what we're doing, and not add to the word or subtract from it. There are a lot of traditions out there, and we have to be careful that we don't trade one set of traditions for another.

As an example to clarify my point, I'm going to review the "Feast of Unleavened Bread."

Note - Mitsrayim means 'Egypt' in the following scripture

Exodus 12:14-20 *'And this day shall become to you a remembrance. And you shall observe it as a festival to YHWH throughout your generations – observe it as a festival, an everlasting law. 'Seven days you shall eat unleavened bread. Indeed on the first day you cause leaven to cease from your houses. For whoever eats leavened bread from the first day until the seventh day, that being shall be cut off from Israel. 'And on the first day is a set-apart gathering, and on the seventh day you have a set-apart gathering. No work at all is done on them, only that which is eaten by every being, that alone is prepared by you. 'And you shall guard the Festival of Unleavened Bread, for on this same day I brought your divisions out of the land of Mitsrayim. And you shall guard this day throughout your generations, an everlasting law. 'In the first month, on the fourteenth day of the month, in the evening, you shall eat unleavened bread until the twenty-first day of the month in the evening. 'For seven days no leaven is to be found in your houses, for if anyone eats what is leavened, that same being shall be cut off from the congregation of Israel, whether sojourner or native of the land. 'Do not eat that which is leavened – in all your dwellings you are to eat unleavened bread.' "*

After this command of the feast was given, the people killed the Passover lambs and spread the blood on the doorposts of their homes. All who did not in Egypt had their firstborns die, and there was not one household where there was not one found dead.

Exodus 12:33-39 *And the Mitsrites urged the people, to hasten to send them away out of the land. For they said, "We are all dying!" And the people took their dough before it was* *leavened, having their kneading bowls bound up in their garments on their shoulders. And the children of Israel had done according to the word of Mosheh, and they had asked from the Mitsrites objects of silver, and objects of gold, and garments. And YHWH gave the people favour in the eyes of the Mitsrites, so that they gave them what they asked, and they plundered the Mitsrites. And the children of Israel set out from Ra`meses to Sukkoth, about six hundred thousand men on foot, besides the little ones. And a mixed multitude went up with them too, also flocks and herds, very much livestock. And they baked unleavened cakes of the dough which they had brought out of Mitsrayim, for it was not leavened, since they were driven out of Mitsrayim, and had not been able to delay, nor had they prepared food for themselves.*

Then YHWH speaks again to Moses:

Exodus 13:1-10 *And YHWH spoke to Mosheh, saying, "Set apart to Me all the first-born, the one opening the womb among the children of Israel, among man and among beast, it is Mine." And Mosheh said to the people, "Remember this day in which you went out of Mitsrayim, out of the house of slavery. For by strength of hand YHWH brought you out of this place, and whatever is leavened shall not be eaten. "Today you are going out, in the month Aḇiḇ. "And it shall be, when YHWH brings you into the land of the Kena`anites, and the Ḥittites, and the Amorites, and the Ḥiwwites, and the Yeḇusites, which He swore to your fathers to give you, a land flowing with milk and honey, that you shall keep this service in this month. "Seven days you eat unleavened bread, and on the seventh day is a festival to YHWH. "Unleavened bread is to be eaten the seven days, and whatever is leavened is not* *to be seen with you, and leaven is not to be seen with you within all your border. "And you shall inform your son in that day, saying, 'It is because of what YHWH did for me when I came up from Mitsrayim.' "And it shall be as a sign to you on your hand and as a reminder between your eyes, that the Torah of YHWH is to be in your mouth, for with a strong hand YHWH has brought you out of Mitsrayim. "And you shall guard this law at its appointed time from year to year.*

Obviously, back in those days, people did not run to the store and buy packets of dried yeast. Yeast was acquired in one of two ways - from pinching a little from a piece of dough that was leavened, or leaving it sitting out to where yeast would get to it from being in the air. When the children of Israel left Egypt in a hurry, they took their kneading troughs with them but they had no time to get a pinch of dough to bring with them.

We are told to get ALL the <u>leaven</u> out of our homes, and to eat unleaven bread for a whole week during that feast. The leaven is **yeast**. A little bit of leaven can leaven the whole lump, as in the lump of dough as it sits warming on your counter, rising and expanding before you bake it. Some people remove baking soda (sodium bicarbonate) from their homes, but this is not leaven. It will only make your bread puff up while it is baking. It will not make your "whole lump" rise as it sits on the kitchen counter as yeast will do. A little bit of baking soda will not "leaven the whole lump." Yeast is living organisms; baking soda is not. Yeast can be acquired by leaving the dough out in the world for a time, but baking soda will not be acquired in this way.

Below is a list of other things that are traditionally done by some people prior to the Feast of Unleavened Bread:

1. Utensils are put away that are used during the rest of the year. Only special utensils for Passover week may be used.

2. "Kashering" of stoves, refrigerators and microwaves. This is to remove any traces of possible crumbs.

It is customary to turn off the lights and conduct the search by candlelight, using a feather and a wooden spoon: candlelight effectively illuminates corners without casting shadows; the feather can dust crumbs out of their hiding places; and the wooden spoon which collects the crumbs can be burned the next day with the chametz.

Because the house is assumed to have been thoroughly cleaned by the night before Passover, there is some concern that making a blessing over the search for chametz will be in vain if nothing is found. So, 10 morsels of bread smaller than the size of an olive can be traditionally hidden throughout the house in order to ensure that some chametz will be found. These are placed in a bag and burned the next morning.

3. Some keep a Passover "seder," where different wine is drank from four different cups in a traditional 15-part ceremony. (This is in direct opposition to Exodus 12:11, which tells us "And thus shall ye eat it; your loins girded, your shoes on your feet, and your staff in your hand; and ye shall eat it in haste: it is YHWH's passover.")

4. Some Jews will say that non-Jews may not partake of the Passover or the Feast of Unleavened bread. In truth, however, those who may observe Passover are those who comprise Israel, those in covenant. The Jews (tribe of Judah) only represent one of the twelve tribes.

At this point you might be wondering why I wrote about all of this of the Feast of Unleavened Bread?

Look at the above four points. **WHERE IS ANY OF THAT WRITTEN IN EXODUS CHAPTER 12 AND 13?**

IT'S NOT IN THERE.

We need to make sure we understand what we're doing, and not add to the word or subtract from it. This is a commandment after all:

Deuteronomy 4:2 *"Do not add to the Word which I command you, and do not take away from it, so as to guard the commands of YHWH your Elohim which I am commanding you."*

Making sure the crumbs are out of the house is a good idea, even to the point of shaking out the toaster. But, re-read point #1 above and examine this again from scripture:

Exodus 12:34 *And the people took their dough before it was leavened, having their kneading bowls bound up in their garments on their shoulders.*

Where would these people get new bowls in the wilderness? Do you suppose they made new bread in the old bread bowls? And as for point #4, The tribe of Yehudah (where we get the name "Jew") was only one tribe out of the twelve tribes of Israel that were present when the commands for this moed were given. Where do they get the idea that people need to be "Jewish" to partake of this feast? That's ridiculous and **NOT** what scripture says.

Who knows where this "seder" idea came from, but that is also adding to the word as well and breaking the commandment.

Can you see the irony of this?

Here is the beginning of the year, where we are to get the "leaven" out of our word, leaven representing traditions and false doctrines, and some people think they can keep this feast by using **tradition and false doctrine**?

THEY MISS THE WHOLE POINT OF THIS FEAST!

What I wanted to show readers in that review was that we should not miss the point of the Shemitah, either. Let us not add to the word or subtract from it, but prayerfully ask Elohim to show us what he requires in order for us to correctly observe his Shemitah.

We've just discussed some of the traditions that add to, take away from, or violate the Feast of Unleavened Bread. The reader will have taken note by now that this book is about <u>obeying</u> the word of YHWH and not living by the traditions of men. That is our only intent, to give to the reader a good, solid source of scriptural truth on how to keep YHWH's Sabbatical rest of the land.

If one gets on the internet and tries to learn more about the Shemitah year, one will find almost nothing out there but terrible misinformation due to "Jewish tradition" that unfortunately causes people to violate the commands regarding the Shemitah in some of the same ways as they do the Feast of Unleavened Bread.

The following is typical information found on the web, and was found on a single website designed as "*A guide to keeping the Shemitah year.*" Please see the corresponding footnotes below.

During the nineteenth century, when Jews began resettling the land in significant numbers, the population was almost starving. Because of this, many rabbinic leaders endorsed the sale of Jewish-owned land to non-Jews for the duration of the Shemitah year. **[1]**

Many believe that while one is not permitted to sell land in Israel to a non-Jew, if the sale will help Israel that it is permissible. Another solution endorsed by many rabbis, is leasing, instead of selling the land for a year.

Yet another complication is that the farmer not only has to sell the land, he also needs to hire non-Jewish workers to perform the prohibited activities. However, some rabbis permit Jewish farmers to engage in rabbi-prohibited activities on non-Jewish owned land. **[2]**

The laws of Shemitah only apply in "The State of Israel." Thus, Shemitah isn't necessarily applicable to all parts of modern-day Israel. Eilat, for example, isn't part of the actual "State" of Israel and thereby one may plant and harvest their own produce there during Shemitah. **[3]**

The Shemitah is a Biblical commandment; however, the rabbis say the Biblical obligation is only in effect when a majority of the Jewish people live in the Land of Israel. Also, some Jewish authorities will say that that Shemitah only has the status of a Biblical commandment when there is a functioning Sanhedrin which is the authoritative court in Jerusalem. **[4]**

Which activities are forbidden during the shemittah year?

The Jewish "sages" forbid the consumption of all annual plants that sprout or came up of their own during the Sabbatical year. **[5]**

Shemitah restrictions don't apply to the plants that are grown indoors in pots or containers without holes in the bottom. Additionally, different techniques of mass growing in special greenhouses has become another popular way to circumvent the commandments of the Shemitah. **[6]**

Because of its 'special status,' the Shemitah produce must be treated with respect. This produce cannot be wasted. The edible left over food, including edible peels of produce like apples and cucumbers, cannot be simply tossed out. The peels of fruits which are inedible are allowed to be discarded. The leftovers that can't be discarded should rot first, and then they be thrown away. There are other opinions that say these leftovers can simply be double wrapped, and then they may be discarded. **[7]**

A further restriction with some Shemitah produce is that an item cannot be cooked that is usually eaten raw (as fruit) nor is it allowed to eat an item raw that is usually cooked. **[8]**

It is very important to remember that someone may not purchase Shemitah produce. When Shemitah produce is purchased, any money used in that transaction will attain a "holy status" as well. This "holy money" may not be used to purchase anything else. **[9]**

Also, Shemitah produce cannot be taken out of Israel. This means that if you buy a bottle of wine, it will have the status of being made during the Shemitah year, whether it actually was or not. Make sure to drink it in Israel and not bring it home with you if you live outside of Israel. However, if you mistakenly bring it home, you are allowed to drink it. **[10]**

The Shemitah begins in the fall, and continues to the fall of the following year. **[11]**

1. So they were tested and failed. And from then on, they attempted to find ways to circumvent the Shemitah instead of having faith in YHWH and His word.

2. You can't hire someone to break the Torah for you.

3. Because if you don't live "in the land of Israel" you can simply disregard all of the commandments? Is this what they actually believe?

4. Is it any wonder the Messiah said; **Matthew 15:9** *'But in vain do they worship Me, teaching for doctrines the commands of men.'*

5. Scriptures tells us the opposite. We cannot "harvest," be we are allowed to eat what grows of itself as long as we don't gather more than what we need for a day's meal (as in the example of the gathering of manna). **Leviticus 25:4-7**

6. The last ten words of this one tells you ALL you need to know in regards to why they do what they do.

7. Chapter and verse please. Can you see how they make up their own rules and follow those instead of what YHWH commands?

8. Chapter and verse please. What part of "*You shall not add to the word*" don't they understand?

9. Read the first sentence of that paragraph and the first 5 words of the second sentence. See any issues there? Also, chapter and verse please regarding "holy money."

10. Wow. This is just so far from what YHWH commanded.

11. The opposite of what YHWH commands, which is from the spring to the following spring. **Exodus 12:2** (One can see that, in context, this verse is talking about the first month of the year being in the spring.) The Jewish Rosh Hashanah, what they consider the start of their new year, they observe on the first day of the seventh biblical month and so in the autumn, and is just another Jewish tradition with absolutely no scriptural support.

Do you see how utterly and completely disobedient one would be to observe the Shemitah in this way? Why would one even bother? It would not please YHWH at all.

What follows is <u>my opinion</u> on this matter. Always take the word of YHWH over my word or anyone else's, for that matter. Prayerfully ask the Father to reveal his will to you, so that you may be obedient in **ALL** things.

My wife Gina and I both know that we are not to sow any seed or preserve foods during the Shemitah. We can pick what grows of its own for a meal, but we should also give some of that away to people in need, and let the animals eat from it. I have removed the fencing from our garden areas to let the rabbits and other wild animals in so they may eat what grows there.

I do not spray our fruit trees with insect repellent, but if I did, I would not during the Shemitah year. I will cut my grass, as we don't eat the grass, of course. I will not prune my grape, muscadine or raspberry vines, however.

I have heard of some people stocking up on toilet paper and paper towels, since they are made from the wood that is harvested from the land. This is true, but how far do we go with this? And how do we know our choices are accurate?

For example, how do we know whether the paper harvested was harvested in the Shemitah year or not? What if it sat in a warehouse for a year before it made it to the store? Could you buy a box of nails, because the iron to make them is mined from the earth? Could you cash your paycheck at the bank and get freshly made bills made with paper and cotton? What if you were handed new copper pennies? Could you buy Q-tips? What about cotton clothing, socks or underwear? Feminine products? You wouldn't want paper bags at the grocery store, but plastic comes from petroleum products pumped from the ground, as does oil and gasoline. Many ingredients in makeup, vitamins, etc. are derived from petroleum. The list goes on and on.

See how far we could go with this?

Let's compare this to manna.

Exodus 16:1 *And they set out from Elim, and all the congregation of the children of Israel came to the Wilderness of Sin, which is between Elim and Sinai, on the fifteenth day of the second month after their going out of the land of Mitsrayim. And all the congregation of the children of Israel grumbled against Mosheh and Aharon in the wilderness. And the children of Israel said to them, "If only we had died by the hand of YHWH in the land of Mitsrayim, when we sat by the pots of meat and when we ate bread to satisfaction! For you have brought us out into this wilderness to put all this assembly to death with hunger." And YHWH said to Mosheh, "See, I am raining bread from the heavens for you. And the people shall go out and gather a day's portion every day, in order to try them, whether they walk in My Torah or not. "And it shall be on the sixth day that they shall prepare what they bring in, and it shall be twice as much as they gather daily."*

Exodus 16:22-26 *And it came to be, on the sixth day, that they gathered twice as much bread, two omers for each one. And all the rulers of the congregation came and told Mosheh. And he said to them, "This is what YHWH has said, 'Tomorrow is a rest, a Sabbath set-apart to YHWH. That which you bake, bake; and that which you cook, cook. And lay up for yourselves all that is left over, to keep it until morning.'" And they laid it up till morning, as Mosheh commanded. And it did not stink, and no worm was in it. And Mosheh said, "Eat it today, for today is a Sabbath to YHWH, today you do not find it in the field. "Gather it six days, but on the seventh day, which is the Sabbath, there is none."*

We work for six days and rest on the seventh. And we work the land for six years and let it rest on the seventh. We gather our crops for six years, and in the sixth year (preparation year) we gather twice as much to hold us over for the Shemitah year.

Consider the following. Man is told to rest every seven days throughout the year, but the land continues to "work" all year long. However, the number of Sabbaths in seven years (364) is equal to the number of days during Shemitah year in which the land is allowed to rest. According to YHWH's plan, when we are obedient to him in our stewardship of the land by keeping the Shemitah, he makes up for the Sabbaths that are missed during the first six years of the cycle and the land gets its rest after all.

Not everyone who reads this book may think that they need to keep the Shemitah in order to be obedient. So I feel that I should address that, to show that we most certainly **DO** need to observe it.

The land will get its rest, and if we don't let it rest then we will be removed from it:

2 Chronicles 36:20-21 *And those who escaped from the sword he exiled to Babel, where they became servants to him and his sons until the reign of the reign of Persia, in order to fill the word of YHWH by the mouth of Jeremiah, until the land had enjoyed her Sabbaths. As long as she lay waste she kept Sabbath, until seventy years were completed.*

This is what YHWH told them would happen to them if they did not obey:

Leviticus 26:33-35 *And I will scatter you among the heathen, and will draw out a sword after you: and your land shall be desolate, and your cities waste. Then shall the land enjoy her sabbaths, as long as it lieth desolate, and you be in your enemies' land; even then shall the land rest, and enjoy her sabbaths. As long as it lies desolate it shall rest; because it did not rest in your sabbaths, when you dwelt upon it.*

Some who have acquired this book may be wondering, "Aren't we supposed to let the land rest only if we live in Israel?" That's a good question and one that is quite common, so next I will present the chapter on this issue from my book "Exit Babylon," to give the answer for those who would ask.

Can we opt out of keeping the Shemitah years if we don't live in the land of Israel?

Have you noticed how many times people will say we don't have to do something YHWH has commanded of his people, because he hasn't brought us "*into the land*" yet?

Does "into the land" always refer to the promised land, the land of our inheritance, or Israel itself?

Let's see what other places the scriptures refer to as being "in the land:"

Genesis 21:32 *Thus they made a covenant at Beersheba: then Abimelech rose up, and Phichol the chief captain of his host, and they returned into the land of the Philistines.*

Genesis 22:2 *And he said, Take now thy son, thine only son Isaac, whom thou lovest, and get thee into the land of Moriah; and offer him there for a burnt offering upon one of the mountains which I will tell thee of.*

Genesis 29:1 *Then Jacob went on his journey, and came into the land of the people of the east.*

Genesis 45:25 *And they went up out of Egypt, and came into the land of Canaan unto Jacob their father,*

Genesis 46:28 *And he sent Judah before him unto Joseph, to direct his face unto Goshen; and they came <u>into the land</u> of Goshen.*

Joshua_24:8 *And I brought you <u>into the land</u> of the Amorites, which dwelt on the other side Jordan;*

Judges 1:26 *And the man went <u>into the land</u> of the Hittites, and built a city,*

1 Samuel 22:5 *And the prophet Gad said unto David, Abide not in the hold; depart, and get thee <u>into the land</u> of Judah.*

1 Samuel 27:1 *there is nothing better for me than that I should speedily escape <u>into the land</u> of the Philistines;*

2 Kings 6:23 *So the bands of Syria came no more <u>into the land</u> of Israel.*

2 Kings 19:37 *Adrammelech and Sharezer his sons smote him with the sword: and they escaped <u>into the land</u> of Armenia.*

1 Chronicles 19:2 *So the servants of David came <u>into the land</u> of the children of Ammon to Hanun, to comfort him.*

Jeremiah 24:5 *Thus saith YHWH the Elohim of Israel; Like these good figs, so will I acknowledge them that are carried away captive of Judah, whom I have sent out of this place <u>into the land</u> of the Chaldeans for their good.*

Jeremiah 37:12 *Then Jeremiah went forth out of Jerusalem to go <u>into the land</u> of Benjamin, to separate himself thence in the midst of the people.*

Jeremiah 43:7 *So they came <u>into the land</u> of Egypt: for they obeyed not the voice of YHWH thus came they even to Tahpanhes.*

Zechariah 10:10 *I will bring them again also out of the land of Egypt, and gather them out of Assyria; and I will bring them <u>into the land</u> of Gilead and Lebanon;*

Matthew 14:34 *And when they were gone over, they came <u>into the land</u> of Gennesaret.*

"Into the land" simply means "a place where people lived."

When YHWH was leading Israel out of Egypt and through the desert, he kept telling them "*When you come into the land...*" They were not in any land yet but in the wilderness where he was training them and providing for them.

Exodus 13:11 "*And it shall be when YHWH shall bring you <u>into the land</u> of the Canaanites, as he swore unto you and to your fathers, and shall give it you*"

YHWH was leading them to a land where the Canaanites resided at the time, to give it to Israel.

We have to remember that this was **ALL** of YHWH's people back then. The Creator was leading all of them to a single place and telling them what they will do when they are no longer "wandering in the desert," but have a land to call their own.

Today, those of us who are his and who are in covenant with him, are scattered to the four corners of the Earth, from where it is written that he will "gather his elect."

Mark 13:27 *"And then He shall send His messengers, and assemble His chosen ones from the four winds, from the farthest part of earth to the farthest part of heaven*."

YHWH gave comandments for his people for when they stopped wandering and were living where he brought them;

Leviticus 19:23 *And when <u>you come into the land</u>*

Leviticus 19:26 *Do not eat meat with the blood. Do not practise divination or magic*
Leviticus 19:28 *And do not make any cuttings in your flesh for the dead*
Leviticus 19:29 *Do not profane your daughter by making her a whore*
Leviticus 19:30 *Guard My Sabbaths*

Deuteronomy 18:9 *When you are come <u>into the land</u> which YHWH your Elohim gives you, you shall not learn to do after the abominations of those nations.*

Does this mean that since we are not living in Israel or that we have not "come into the land" that we can do the abominations of other nations, eat blood, use enchantment, cut our flesh for the dead, or that it's OK to whore out our daughters and break the Sabbaths?

Of course not.

That means this still stands:

Leviticus 25:2 *Speak unto the children of Israel, and say unto them, When you come <u>into the land</u> which I give you,* ***then shall the land keep a sabbath unto YHWH.***

As does this:

Numbers 9:9-10 *And YHWH spake unto Moses, saying, Speak unto the children of Israel, saying, If any man of you or of your posterity shall be unclean by reason of a dead body, or be in a journey afar off, yet he shall keep the passover unto YHWH.*

Even if someone was in a journey far away from "the land," they were commanded to still keep the Passover to YHWH.

Everyone reading this is living in the land. It is either the land you were born in, or the land you moved to. <u>We do not get to go into the promised land/our inheritance until YHWH puts</u>

us there. Until that time, we are "in the land" and must do as YHWH commands us.

Deuteronomy 28:1 *And it shall come to pass, if you shall hearken diligently unto the voice of YHWH thy Elohim, to observe and to do all his commandments which I command you this day,*

(Remember at this point they were not in their land yet)

Deuteronomy 11:22-24 *For if you shall diligently keep all these commandments which I command you, to do them, to love YHWH your Elohim, to walk in **all his ways**, and to cleave unto him;   Then will YHWH drive out all these nations from before you, and you shall possess greater nations and mightier than yourselves. **Every place whereon the soles of your feet shall tread shall be yours:** from the wilderness and Lebanon, from the river, the river Euphrates, even unto the uttermost sea shall your coast be.*

Is YHWH going to have different sets of rules for his people "In the land" of Israel, as opposed to in other parts of the Earth?

YHWH is not a respecter of persons, correct? Do we all have the same commandments? Wasn't the "Good News" the fact that people could return to the covenant (after the death and resurrection of the Messiah) by keeping it where they had been presently scattered?

Are we not told to take stewardship of the land, take care of it and be a light to the nations where we have been scattered?

So wouldn't we show our fruit and be a light by letting the land rest where we are now? Wouldn't that make an excellent statement of our faith in YHWH and His Word?!?!

YHWH said "*If you diligently obey and **DO ALL** that I command.*"

When YHWH led his people through the wilderness, he told them to gather manna for six days but not on the Shabbat. He told them to gather twice as much on the 6th day (preparation day), to last them for two days, for the 6th day and for the Shabbat, and that it would not spoil. He was testing them and training them. He tells us to sow our land and harvest for six years, but let it rest on the seventh year. He instructs us to grow twice as much on the 6th year to last for two years, the 6th year as well as the shemitah. This is also a test for us. Do we have faith that we can make it for the seventh year?

And we are instructed to read the ENTIRE COVENANT out loud to the people on that shemitah (Sabbatical) year, is this still not a good idea? It's a commandment! It re-confirms our covenant oaths that we are YHWH's people! The year of rest for the land models the day of rest for the people. We read his Torah covenant out loud to all in the body, as we are to worship him in spirit and truth on the Sabbath day and in the Sabbatical years. They are a sign that we are his people!

Deuteronomy 31:10-12 *And Moses commanded them, saying, At the end of every seven years, in the solemnity of the year of release, in the <u>feast of tabernacles</u>, When all Israel is come to appear before YHWH your Elohim in the* *place which he shall choose, you shall read this Torah before all Israel in their hearing. Gather the people together, men, and women, and children, and thy stranger that is within your gates, that they may hear, and that they may learn, and fear YHWH your Elohim, and observe to do all the words of this Torah*

Do we not keep the Feast of Tabernacles here? The Shabbat? Why would we not keep the Shemitah year as well? The Shemitah is just as important as the Shabbat!!

We count the omer for 49 days, and the 50th day is Shavuot. 7 Shabbats times 7 Shabbats = Shavuot.

We count 49 years, and the 50th is the jubilee year. 7 Sabbatical years times 7 Sabbatical years = Jubilee.

We work 6 days and rest for the 7th. We work our land for 6 years and let it rest on the 7th.

These are perfect cycles which YHWH set up to refresh us AND the land.

The moon is refreshed every month, the cycle of stars in the heavens is refreshed every year, and wherever we are on the Earth, we can use these for our timepieces to be on YHWH's scheduled time for moedim. Everything fits together perfectly.

To say that we do not let our land rest because we are not "In the land of Israel" does not make sense. It sounds like people are making excuses for not obeying, or saying "*Yeah, we don't have to do that stuff because we don't live in Israel.*" Is that just an another excuse to **NOT** obey Elohim?

Remember when YHWH said he would bring "curses to your land?" Seven Sabbatical years times seven Sabbatical years marks the year of Jubilee. If we don't keep those Shemitah years, could that be why he says "*I will curse you **seven times**???*"

The land doesn't get a weekly Shabbat like we do. It misses 52 Sabbath days a year, but if you multiply that by seven years for the Shemitah/Sabbatical cycle, you come up with 364 days. Coincidence? No, it means that the land will rest for one full year. It's YHWH perfect cycle.

We are commanded in the commandment for the Shabbat that; "*the seventh day is the Sabbath of YHWH your Elohim: in it you shall not do any work, you, nor your son, nor your daughter, your manservant, nor your maidservant, nor your cattle, nor your stranger that is within your gates*" (**Exodus 20:10**)

The end of that verse says that neither your cattle nor a stranger (Goyim) within your gates would know to keep the Shabbat, and that you will not cause them to work. In that same way we are to be active to prevent our land from work during the Shemitah year.

You can look in one of the above scripture references and say "*Yes, but look; it says 'in the place that he shall choose'.*" Correct. Once again, remember that they were wandering in the wilderness and did not have a land to live in yet as they were being trained by YHWH *for when they did*. Except for very few others (groups being lead by Balaam up until his apostasy, and possibly by Yitro, Moshe's father in law who many believe was "converted" from his pagan ways), there were no other groups of people who were "in-covenant with YHWH" in any other lands on the Earth. The children of Israel were in the wilderness in a single group or body, being led by YHWH and taught by Moses. YHWH knew that they would fail to keep the covenant and would end up being scattered. Because of this, he told them how to come back when they had been cast among the gentiles.

It is written that "*The elect will be gathered from the four corners of the Earth*". **It doesn't say** they will only be gathered "from the land of Israel only."

Are we not all supposed to be led by YHWH together? Are we not all **ONE BODY**? Is there only **ONE** covenant? **ONE** Torah for all?

Are we not to "diligently obey **ALL**" that YHWH said?

We are told to choose blessing or curses -

Deuteronomy 30:19 *I call heaven and earth to record this day against you, that I have set before you life and death, blessing and cursing: therefore choose life, that both you and your seed may live*

Our blessings are evident in our obedience to the Torah, and our curses are evident in our disobedience. **YHWH calls Heaven and Earth to bear witness against us**, and so would our land being hard and our skies being without rain not be the heaven and Earth bearing witness against our disobedience?

LITERALLY!

Blessings are evident in the **heavens and Earth bearing witness:**

Leviticus 26:4 *Then I will give you rain in due season, and the land shall yield her increase, and the trees of the field shall yield their fruit.*

Curses are evident in the **heavens and Earth bearing witness:**

Leviticus 26:19 *And I will break the pride of your power; and I will make your heaven as iron, and your earth as brass:*

The fruitfulness of the land to which we are custodian will be **according to our obedience** to the Torah and Shemitah years!!

More scripture with highlighted parts of Leviticus 26, which is all about the Shemitah year:

Leviticus 26:2 *You shall keep my sabbaths, and reverence my sanctuary: I am YHWH.*

Leviticus 26:3 *If you walk in my statutes, and keep my commandments, and do them;*

Leviticus 26:4 ***Then I will give you rain in due season, and the land shall yield her increase, and the trees of the field shall yield their fruit.***

Leviticus 26:5 ***And your threshing shall reach unto the vintage, and the vintage shall reach unto the sowing time: and you shall eat your bread to the full, and dwell in your land safely.***

Leviticus 26:9 *For I will have respect unto you, and make you fruitful, and multiply you, and establish my covenant with you.*

Leviticus 26:10 ***And you shall eat old store, and bring forth the old because of the new.***

Leviticus26:14 *But if you will not hearken unto me, and will not do all these commandments;*

Leviticus26:15 *And if you shall despise my statutes, or if your soul abhor my judgments, so that you will not do all my commandments, but that you break my covenant:*

Leviticus26:16 *I also will do this unto you; I will even appoint over you terror, consumption, and the burning ague, that* *shall consume the eyes, and cause sorrow of heart:* **and you shall sow your seed in vain, for your enemies shall eat it.**

Leviticus 26:19 *And I will break the pride of your power; and I will make your heaven as iron, and* **your earth as brass:**

Leviticus 26:20 *And your strength shall be spent in vain: for* **your land shall not yield her increase, neither shall the trees of the land yield their fruits.**

Leviticus 26:21 *And if you walk contrary unto me, and will not hearken unto me;* **I will bring seven times more plagues upon you according to your sins.**

Leviticus 26:23 *And if you will not be reformed by me by these things, but will walk contrary unto me;*

Leviticus 26:24 *Then will I also walk contrary unto you, and* **will punish you yet seven times** *for your sins.*

Leviticus26:27 *And if you will not for all this hearken unto me, but walk contrary unto me;*

Leviticus 26:28 *Then I will walk contrary unto you also in fury; and I, even I,* **will chastise you seven times for your sins.**

Leviticus26:29 *And you shall eat the flesh of your sons, and the flesh of your daughters shall you eat.*

Leviticus 26:32 **And I will bring the land into desolation**: *and your enemies which dwell therein shall be astonished at it.*

Leviticus 26:33 *And I will scatter you among the heathen, and will draw out a sword after you: and your* **land shall be**

desolate, and your cities waste.

Leviticus 26:34 *Then shall the land enjoy her sabbaths, as long as it lieth desolate, and you be in your enemies' land; even then shall the land rest, and enjoy her sabbaths.*

Leviticus 26:35 As long as it lies desolate it shall rest; because it did not rest in your sabbaths, when you dwelt upon it.

Pay close attention to this next part, as this should remove all doubt.

Deuteronomy 30:1 *And it shall come to pass, when all these things are come upon you, the blessing and the curse, which I have set before you, <u>**and you shall call them to mind among all the nations, where YHWH your Elohim has driven you**</u>,*

(At this point the reader has been driven into some other nation, and can call all of these instructions to his mind while there)

Deuteronomy 30:2 *And shall return unto YHWH your Elohim, and shall obey his voice according to all that I command you this day*, you and your children, with all your heart, and with all your soul;

(The reader will then return to ALL of the instructions and obey <u>ALL</u> that the Creator told the people **back then ON <u>THAT DAY</u>**)

Deuteronomy 30:3 *That **then YHWH your Elohim will turn your captivity, and have compassion upon you, and will return and gather you from all the nations,** where YHWH your Elohim has scattered you.*

THEN will YHWH have compassion on you for your obedience and re-gather you for being obedient to him in ALL things.

IF WE KEEP THE SABBATICAL YEARS (along with all of the Torah) WHILE IN THE DIASPORA, THEN YHWH WILL REGATHER US TO THE LAND, **proving we don't have to be in the land in the first place in order to keep the Sabbatical years!**

We can eat what our land produces on its own during Shemitah, such as produce from our older berry or fruit trees, or lettuce or beans, for example that may seed themselves. We cannot "harvest" or store these foods as we let the land rest, but we can water our new trees or fertilize them, so we definitely plan on doing that.

A couple years ago, before we ever knew we'd be observing a Shemitah year, we planted several different fruit trees and bushes. We planted three Alberta peach trees, six Rabbiteye blueberry bushes, some hazelnut trees, and a small mulberry tree orchard.

According to the Torah (Leviticus 19:23-25), we cannot eat of these trees until the fifth year, so by the next Shemitah prep year, all of these fruit trees will figure prominently into our food preps. We also hope to plant a couple more apple trees and a fig tree the year after the Shemitah, so those we can gather of in the next Shemitah prep year as well.

Don't make the same mistakes I did; research what does best in your area. We are not natives of the area in which we now live. We moved 850 miles to relocate here. I simply went to a garden center at a popular discount store and bought fruit trees that were on sale and I planted them. Unfortunately, their corporate office has them sell the same type of fruit trees for their stores in Maine, Florida, Washington State and California, so most of ours did not make it. I took for granted that if they sold them here they were meant to flourish here.

WRONG.

In preparation for the Shemitah, go to local growers, members of your local farmers' market and nurseries and get advice from them. Learn how to fertilize, mulch, and prune. Neighbors and friends in your area who have experience can provide a great wealth of information.

Here's a great example of what friends in the area gave us, what they knew would grow and produce well in our location.

Seeds to grow "Rattlesnake" green beans.

These beans are planted in the spring just like ordinary green beans, and they start to grow and look just like them. Our friends told us one thing about these beans though - prepare for CRAZY amounts of them. Also, they advised us to build some sort of "tripod" for them to grow on, like a trellis of sorts. They said if we planted them at the base of a 60 foot oak tree that they would grow to the very top of the tree because the vines were that intense!

I didn't feel like climbing to the tops of my trees to harvest our green beans, so I opted for the tripod plan instead. For this I decided I would build two of them, each out of three pieces of ten foot long and one inch diameter electrical thinwall pipe (EMT). I drilled a hole in the ends of them, and tied three together with strong wire and erected them like teepees in the yard. Then I drove stakes where the pipes sat on the ground and wired them down so they wouldn't blow over in a gust of wind or a storm.

Then I planted six bean seeds at the base of each pipe, and wrapped two foot tall circles of chicken wire around the pipes to protect the young beans sprouts from our excessive rabbit population. Gina raked the grass clippings and spread them around the chicken wire to help hold in moisture, as the ground was rather rocky where we had to plant them. This helped quite a bit during the dry summer months.

One tripod leg, showing the chicken wire wrap and the grass clippings around it.

The vines climbed to the top quickly, so I tied a rope between the two tripods to give them more room to travel, which they did. We picked an early crop of a few beans, and then they went almost dormant for a couple months. Then they went crazy, and every day we picked so many we eventually had to quit picking and blanching them because the freezer was full.

That's a full size lawn chair sitting under the rope between our bean tripods!

Speaking of blanching green beans and freezing them, they last MUCH longer if you put them in a deep freeze that is not "frost free." These will be the freezers that you have to get the ice out of them by thawing slightly then removing large chunks of it every few years when it builds up in them. The frost-free freezers tend to "freezer burn" the foods and dry them out. Most, if not all refrigerators today have frost-free freezers built in. This is fine for short periods of time; just beware of these for long-term storage.

We like to blanch the beans, put them in large plastic zipping freezer bags and squeeze out all the air before we seal them up. Then we write the dates sealed on the bags, put them in large plastic bags for extra protection, and then wrap them snugly in old, clean large towels to really extend freezer life. We can usually get these to store just fine for 18 months, which is what you would need from time of late harvest until the Shemitah year is over.

A neighbor of ours gave us a wonderful tip we had never heard of before – planting crops in holes in old carpets on the ground in your garden.

This sounds very bizarre, but let me explain. Because it was PHENOMENAL.

Find some old carpet you can afford to ruin, preferably of a lighter color that will not absorb the hot rays of the sun like a dark color will. Sometimes people who are replacing carpet in their homes will be delighted to let you have their old carpet for free, so they don't have to haul it off and pay to dispose of it someplace.

Prepare a place in your garden to put it. You need not work the soil, but simply cut grass and weeds down to grass level so it allows your carpet to lay flat. I stake it down at each corner and on the sides by cutting a small slit in the carpet and hammering a stake through it on an angle. This way if a storm blows up, it will not get under the carpet and tear it away. After the weeds start to grow, they will help anchor it to the soil as well.

Then you cut 4 inch square holes in the carpet, and this is where you plant your starts. This works best for squash or vining-type plants like yellow summer squash, butternut, zucchini, cucumbers, melons, etc.

I also plant around the edges of the carpets and train the vines to grow on the carpets and not off the edges. I usually plant 3 feet apart in all directions.

Why would you consider doing this? For starters, any area can be a "carpet garden." You just have to keep rabbits out, and we staked these down right over our lawn, next to the main garden. The grass will grow back. In our climate that gets very little rain in the summer and our temps get very high, the carpet holds the moisture in very well. It makes weeding almost a thing of the past, and it makes it very easy to spot what is growing on the carpets so you can keep track of it better. We fertilized lightly with a popular fertilizer used by mixing with water and applying. I put those colored landscaping flags down where I planted each plant. That way when the plants got really tall and thick, I simply watered at the base of the flags if I couldn't see where they were planted, so that I knew the roots were getting watered.

This carpet idea is probably one of the best gardening tips I have ever gotten in my life. I had some plants of the same variety, grown and planted at the same time and watered at the same intervals, on the carpets and off the carpets in a regular garden area. The plants not on the carpets did miserably compared to the carpet areas. We did not get our first hard frost until late November, and I continued picking

Right after some starts were planted in holes in the carpets, and other plants were planted around them.

And how well they were growing, 2.5 weeks later.

produce off of these plants on the carpets until a week before December! They were huge and beautiful.

I eagerly anticipate the year after Shemitah, because I'm doing nothing but carpet gardens and I will have carpets all over the place. The ones I used this year I pulled up, rinsed off, let them dry and rolled them up. They will easily last for another growing season.

Here's another useful tip. During the Shemitah prep year, if you have a little yard, a small lot or a tiny garden, find ways to improvise. The object is to grow enough food to put up (preserve) to sustain your family until the Shemitah is over. Since we cannot just go to the grocery store and buy fruits and vegetables during that year, we need to make use of any space we can to grow food to put up, can, dehydrate, and save. One can easily grow climbing beans or vines on existing barbed wire fences, terrace railings, or even run temporary ropes for use as a trellis. Plant anywhere and everywhere to grow enough for the Shemitah. We also used our flower beds for growing vegetables.

This is only once every seven years that we observe the Shemitah, and hopefully you can put in some fruit trees, berry bushes, asparagus or rhubarb plants that will come in nicely for the next Shemitah preparation year.

ALL the land is supposed to rest, and anyone who is properly observing the Shemitah year should **NOT** consume food grown <u>anywhere</u> during that year. So that rules out "going out to dinner" for us.

We might be able to eat a steak, but not the salad, bread, and I wouldn't even want the parsley put on the plate.

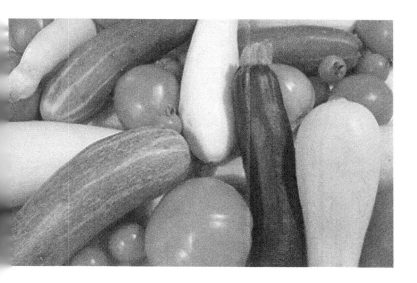

Gina and I give thanks and praise to our Creator for the bounty He let us preserve and put up this year for the Shemitah!

We know there are LOTS of books and websites that talk about canning foods, and that may be something you want to do. We canned many different foods for years and years. Both Gina and I were raised with our mothers doing it and for those who wish to do so - wonderful. We do not discuss canning, pickling, making jellies or jams or those things in this book.

We discovered dehydrating foods a few years ago, and we find it superior in many ways to conventional canning and this is what we are going to discuss in this book. There may be other ways of doing it that we are not aware of, or better ways, or better dehydrators. What we are going to write about is what ***WE*** did and what works for us.

Our two main food dehydrators. The black one on the left is the smallest "Excalibur" dehydrator model they make, a four tray unit that works great. The white one on the right is the Nesco five tray model. (shown with just one tray)

If you get a dehydrator, you're better off buying a new one. Then you'll get the factory warranty, as sometimes the heating elements or fans can burn out as easily as a light bulb. And if you buy one on ebay there's a good chance you won't get the owners' manual either.

The manual will give you some recipes, but more importantly it will give you the correct heat settings for your machine, on what temps to dehydrate different foods. Some of these are printed on the outside of the units – but not always. Or they can wear off easily with use and cleaning.

The lowest temps are for the "living foods" such as herbs and greens, while the highest setting is for meat such as jerky. We like jerky but since you can buy meat, eggs and dairy products during the Shemitah year, I didn't go into those foods in this book.

There's a book available called "***The Dehydrator Bible***" that has over 400 recipes in it; you might want to give that book a try. We just give a sample in this book to give people a rough idea of what can be done with one.

I know quite a few people who freeze everything they grow. What would they do if the power went out for an extended period of time? And what if it was during the Shemitah? You couldn't just run out and "go buy more" at the grocery store of what you had lost if you are being obedient to YHWH and you do not want to violate the Shemitah.

OK, let's get into some dehydrating.

The reality -

For vegetables, don't expect to dehydrate something like corn, then rehydrate it and have the corn be the consistency and texture of fresh corn. That's not going to happen. If you expect to have a mound of rehydrated vegetables on your plate that look fresh cooked from your garden or even appear like re-heated from a can, you've got the wrong impression. Dehydrated vegetables are normally part of a recipe. Stews, soups, breads, casseroles, cakes, pies, home made salad dressings and sauces.

Just as canned corn does not taste nearly as good as corn on the cob, and fresh spinach is so much better than canned spinach, this will be similar to rehydrated vegetables. However, with some rehydrated foods it is difficult to tell the fresh from the rehydrated. We've done cabbage soup with rehydrated cabbage, and it was just as good as fresh. If we had served it to someone without telling them how we prepared it, they would have had no idea it had been done with rehydrated cabbage.

When we make a stuffed turkey, I like to use an old family recipe for stuffing that is made with raisins, sugar, cinammon, and fresh apple slices. We used rehydrated apple slices made from our own apple trees, and it was every bit as good as fresh when cooked. You just need to experiment.

The best part is, you know what you're using as YOU have dehydrated it. No chemicals or preservatives, except a little fresh lemon juice on certain items. Some foods you need more of, as the taste may be a little bland, and some you need less of as the taste will be enhanced. Onions, once dehydrated and rehydrated will be much stronger for some reason. Experiment.

Of course during the Shemitah year, you cannot run out and buy snacks. No potato chips, cookies, pretzels, etc. So if you are a heavy snacker (like me), you need to make your own snacks. Plenty of them. This is preparation for a whole year, remember! But I'll bet if you make healthy snacks from your fruit and vegetables you will be so much healthier by the end of the Shemitah year, and it will be just one more blessing the Father will give you for your obedience!

Some things will dehydrate but won't be great for snacking, such as asparagus. This you'll want to re-hydrate and use for soups and the like.

Once you have your dehydrator, do a little dehydrating experiment. Most people already know they like (or will like) dried/dehydrated fruits, so do an experiment with vegetables, just to see what you like. Go visit your farmer's market or grocery store, and buy a little or one of each of:

Tomato, zucchini, cucumber, yellow or summer squash, some okra, mushroom, radishes, broccoli and cauliflower.

Slice them thin and evenly if you don't have a Mandolin slicer, salt lightly if desired, and dehydrate until brittle and crunchy. See what you think. If you are a vegetable lover like us, you will discover a new taste sensation and realize you will need to dehydrate a LOT of these to satisfy your snacking needs during the Shemitah. Then do a similar experiment with different fruits.

Cabbage works great. I shred it first and it resembles shredded paper when dry. So watch the prices, buy it when it's in season and stock up when the price is right. Lettuce and spinach can't be dehydrated and neither can avocados, but I've had success with everything else I've tried. Some people dehydrate orange slices with the rind on and eat them that way, but they are too bitter for us with the rind so we remove it prior to dehydrating. And they dry much faster that way.

Dried citrus slices are delicious! We rehydrated some dried lime slices, put them on top of salmon as we poached it and it worked every bit as well as fresh limes. The key is soaking them in water for a few hours (or overnight) to rehydrate before using. I did the same with the apple slices for the turkey. We ran short for the recipe as we couldn't stop eating the rehydrated apples!

Once you start doing this it will become a way of life in addition to canning, blanching and freezing or any other type of food preservation you use. There are great plans on the internet and some wonderful videos on You Tube for making large solar dehydrators. I'd love to make one of these and not need electricity for my dehydrating. We've used as many as three dehydrators at one time, and this sure heats up the house when they are all running at once.

We still conventionally can certain foods like pickles, jams and jellies, and that type of thing. Dehydrated foods are so much lighter in weight and can last a very, very long time. I can shred and dehydrate 80 heads of cabbage and lift them all at one time with my little finger. You can mash them down and get 50 heads in a super pail. That's some excellent storage!

So many of the apples on our apple tree used to go to waste every year. But we dehydrated some apple chunk slices for turkey stuffing and apple pies, and some apples we cored, peeled, and sliced into rings. Then we dehydrated some plain, and some with a little sugar and cinnamon, and we were able to preserve a lot of food and snacks from just our single apple tree. Pears work great, too, but they must be ripe to dehydrate properly.

Watermelon and cantaloupe once dehydrated taste like candy. Try some; you'll see.

Once you start dehydrating, what will amaze you right away is the remarkable amount of dehydrated food you can fit in a small space. And since you are only removing the water from the foods – NONE of the nutrients are taken out as if you simply boiled your vegetables. It <u>all stays</u> in your food.

You can fit about eight WHOLE dehydrated tomatoes in the space of one single fresh tomato.

You can eat them like this if you wanted to, but they are very hard and crunchy. I sometimes slice them very thin and add a little sea salt to them before dehydrating, and they are like "tomato chips" instead of potato chips. Delicious! And better for you with no deep frying or added fat/oils like potato chips.

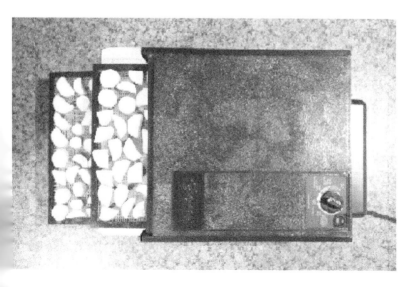

Top view of the Excalibur (with only 2 of the trays pulled out) while yellow squash is dehydrating.

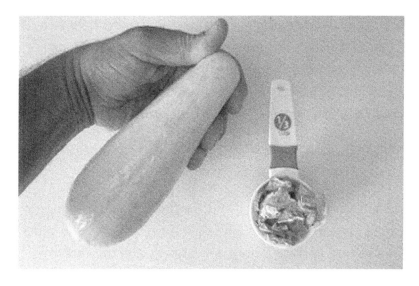

Summer squash or yellow squash. One average large squash that is cut up, cubed, then dehydrated, will yield 1/3 cup.

Some vegatables you can slice or chunk up and dehydrate raw, others you need to cook partially or completely and then dehydrate them. Since this book is not a comprehensive book on dehyrating foods, we are just giving some examples.

We love beef jerky, and made on the dehydrators it's simply the best, but since you can buy meat and make jerky during the Shemitah year, we didn't make any nor will we discuss it further in this book.

This is a photo of the mandolin slicers I use:

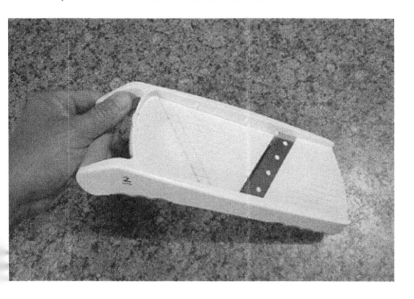

WARNING – Don't use one of these, unless you have this:

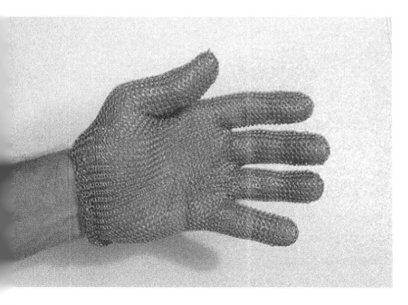

tainless mesh (butchers) glove. You **WILL** cut yourself with
licers – accidents happen. I bought this one used on ebay.

Here's an example of the incredible space-saving feature of dehydrating. I'm holding an average yellow summer squash. **THIRTY of them** *fit in the half gallon jar on the right after dehydrating. Incredible!*

Yellow squash and zucchini can be cut into thick slices or chunks and dehydrated raw to rehydrate later. Cucumbers do not rehydrate well for us; they get very rubbery. So we made chips out of thin slices. With tomatoes you can make chips or they dehydrate well to put in soups or stews later if you chunk them up. Butternut squash needs to be cooked first, but not to the point of being too soft as you need to be able to place it on dehydrator racks without it turning to mush or falling apart. Start experimenting. Research it online; there are many excellent websites devoted to dehydrating vegetables, and don't forget all of the wonderful You Tube videos out there.

*Here's another great example. Six large Butternut squash, once cubed and dehydrated, will **ALL** fit into a single half gallon canning jar.*

When dehydrated, butternut squash will be very hard and almost impossible to break. You need at least 24 hours to rehydrate in your refrigerator, and make sure it stays under the water's surface. If it is not quite rehydrated, it will finish while you are cooking with it.

Just make sure to add a little extra water to your recipe to make up for what this squash will suck up as it finishes rehydrating.

Next, I'd like to add some "how-to" information on growing and dehydrating. I'm also including a couple of recipes. This will show you how we plan to use some of our Shemitah preps.

How to Grow Sweet Potatoes

Most people probably don't realize how easy it is to grow your own sweet potatoes, how well they tolerate growing in high heat and drought-like conditions, how well they keep and the high yield you can get from a single potato.

Someone told me how easy they were to grow, and I decided to find out for myself. I took photos along the way to share my experience with others. This is just an account of how I did it with almost no instruction from anyone, so you may alter it somewhat to fit your needs.

First, I simply purchased a few small sweet potatoes at my local food store. They don't need to be large as you are just acquiring these to grow "starts," as you don't plant the actual potato. I then took an empty 2 liter soda bottle, and cut it down to leave it a little over half size . (fig. 1) This allowed me to see how the rooting progressed over time and made it easier to photograph them.

Fig. 1

Place your potatoes inside, and fill with water to cover them about 3/4 of the way. You don't want to submerge them. (fig. 2) Place on a window sill to give them some light and to watch their progress. I started this about six weeks before I planned on putting them in my garden, enough time to get them ready for planting.

Soon you will see them start to root out, and buds or "starts" will start to form on the tops of them. (fig. 3) Be careful if you handle them as the starts can easily break off at this time. They are similar to "eyes" on red or white potatoes. As the roots come out directly at the bottom of the individual starts over time, make sure you keep the water level just above there, to encourage root growth at the actual starts themselves as this is what you need.

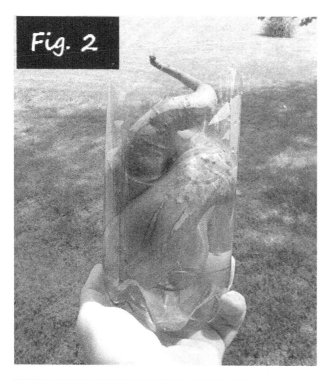

Fig. 2

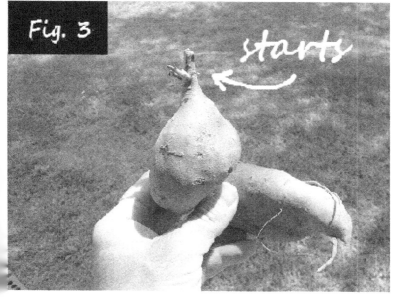

Fig. 3 — *starts*

After six weeks of time, they look very lush as the starts turn into vines and the roots are thick. (fig. 4) Keep water level maintained as they are really using it up by now, and make sure they get a lot of sun in the window area where you have them. At this point you can either transplant them into their own small containers to let them grow a little larger, or plant them directly into your garden.

The soil needs to be a warm temperature for planting. If it's too cool outside, wait to plant. In other words, the warmer the soil the better for sweet potatoes. If the soil temperature during the day is below 80 degrees, they probably won't grow.

Prepare a place in your garden for them. They need the soil mixed with sand on a ratio of 1:1. In other words, half soil, half sand. Regular soil is too hard for them to expand and grow in. (However, if you live in an area like south Florida or some other geographic location with sandy soil, you may be fine just planting them directly.)

Dig a hole roughly 16 inches in diameter and two feet deep at the minimum. Mix the soil and sand well. Space 40 inches apart.

Carefully pull your sweet potatoes out of the bottle and separate them. You can see how most of the starts are barely hanging on to the potatoes at this point, with their own healthy vine and hearty root system.

Carefully break a start off the main potato, taking care not to damage the vine or its root network. (fig. 5) Plant this directly into the prepared area, carefully letting the roots drop straight down and backfill carefully. Keep them soaked for the first couple of weeks until they get established.

Once they get established, they tolerate the heat well. Soil temperatures of 90-100 degrees are best for sweet potato growth. Water with the rest of your garden, and the vines will tend to dry up somewhat and by the fall they may break off, but the potatoes will be fine under the ground.

Dig them up carefully before you get your first frost, making sure not to snap them or gouge them with a shovel. They will be clustered together in a large "knot." (fig. 6) Don't scrub them, but take a hose and rinse off the clods of dirt, then place them in an airy container like a milk crate and store in a cool, dark place.

We dug ours up over seven months ago, and they look, feel and taste just as fresh as the day we dug them. Save some of the "straggly" looking ones for next year's crop.

This is what you want to try to get from each plant! The "knot" in figure 6 grew out of one small start, and there can be as many as 20 starts per potato. We got all the sweet potato plants we needed from just a single potato!

Chips, Chips, Chips!

Tired of potato chips? Try "tomato chips!"
Cucumber chips, yellow squash chips, zucchini, apple, pear, etc. All done with raw foods on your dehydrator, all easy and all very healthy.

Buy organic produce (or grow it yourself), and cut the veggies up on the thinnest slice on the mandolin slicer. I lightly sea salt them after placing them on racks, and dehydrate until they shatter. Turn off dehydrator and let them cool for 5 minutes and place in canning jars, lids tightly closed, with desiccants right away (or they will start to absorb humidity in the room) and you don't want to pack them up even slightly damp.

You're not living until you have a bowl of fresh zucchini chips. Picky-eating kids? They will eat THEM ALL. First-hand knowledge here, folks.

Want candy? Do thicker watermelon or muskmelon slices. You won't believe how great it is.

Apple chips are great, whether plain, lightly salted, or dusted with some cinnamon/sugar when first placed on trays. Use an apple peeler and corer to make life easier. Slice thin, soak in a 10/90 solution of lemon juice and water IMMEDIATELY after slicing - or they will turn brown. Soak for 5 minutes, place on racks, sprinkle anything on if desired and dry until brittle.

Same deal with pears.

The Excalibur with flexible drying racks makes it easier to remove the chips when done, as they can stick really badly to other hard trays.

Two dehydrated apple chips from the same apple. The chip on the right was soaked in lemon juice for a few minutes prior to dehydrating, the chip on the left was not. Quite the difference!

Dehydrated Okra

This makes a great snack - even for those who do not like okra. Many people do not like the "sliminess" in cooked okra, but dehydrated okra doesn't have it. Think of egg white spilled on your counter. If you leave it overnight, it will be like 'powder' the next day. Same sort of thing with the okra 'slime' when it's dried.

I use both green and red "Cowhorn" okra. The red gets a little longer, it is a little more tender and won't be as slimy if you fry it instead. It dries up a little smaller though. Get fresh pods that will cut up tender, just like you'd use for cooking.

Okra, fresh picked.

Wash well (but DON'T dry it on a towel or anything), and cut both ends off. If a piece cuts rough and hard - throw it away. It will dehydrate too hard to eat.

Cut down the middle lengthwise, and if the pods are very long, cut them in half to make them shorter. Place them in a large bowl.

I like to add my own "spices" to them to snazz them up a little. What I do is take some dehydrated tomato slices and green pepper slices and put them in a coffee grinder. Pulverize and grind to a powder. There should be about 2 tablespoons of tomato and one tablespoon of green pepper powder. Then I add a tablespoon each of garlic powder, onion powder, sea salt and some fresh ground pepper, about half of a teaspoon. I mix all of this up well and put in an old spice jar beforehand, to sprinkle on the fresh-cut okra.

Right away sprinkle the spices on them and use your hand to mix well, to evenly coat the okra pieces. The slightly wet okra will help the spices stick better. Sprinkle the spices on both sides, but especially try to get a good amount on the inside halves of the pods as it will hold better in there, and not fall or rub off as it will on the outside of the pods while it is in storage.

Sprinkling the prepared spices on the okra. Do only a couple tray's worth at a time.

Place the okra <u>cut side down</u> on the dehydrator trays. I try to pick out the well spiced-up pieces first, and leave any pieces without spices on them for later and then put more spices on at that time, mix well and then keep loading the trays. Repeat this process until your trays are full.

I use a seven-tray Nesco dehydrator for okra, and the spice amounts above should be mostly used up on each batch. As you get some experience with doing this, you will be able to estimate fairly closely how much okra you need to pick to fill all the trays on your dehydrator.

Okra on a Nesco dehydrator rack. Cut side down.
Place the temp at 135 degrees, and leave them on the dehydrator for about 16 hours. They will shatter when done - they will be that dry.

The finished product. Dry, brittle, and delicious!

Let them cool for 30 minutes, and place in canning jars with a small oxygen absorber and a clay desiccant pack. Gently shake the jar to let the dry okra settle so you can fill them up. Seven full Nesco trays will net almost 2 full quarts of dried product.

Can be eaten immediately!

note - for "Chili okra," take 2 large dry Ancho peppers and powder them up (no seeds) in your coffee grinder. Add the salt to it, but cut the garlic and onion powder amounts in half.

These are excellent, and since Ancho peppers are sweet, this chili okra is not spicy hot and just about everyone will love this as well.

* And for "Tomato okra," use powdered tomato almost exclusively as the spices. Add a little garlic powder, onion powder and salt, and these are a whole different flavor of course but very tasty.

Pumpkin Chips

On the dehydrator

During late summer, take advantage of a crop which is available at amazingly low prices, the pumpkin crop. Make sure you get the smaller "cooking pumpkins" or "pie pumpkins," and not the ones people carve for the kids. Save the seeds for snacks (next recipe).

Prepare your spices (if desired) - here is a suggestion;

1 tsp ground cinnamon

1 tsp ground ginger

1/2 tsp ground nutmeg (or mace)

1 tsp ground cloves

1/2 tsp ground allspice

(1/4 cup sugar if desired)

Mix all of these ingredients and place in a shaker to sprinkle on pumpkin slices later.

What to do:

Wash your pumpkin.

Put it in a 300-degree over on a cookie sheet for half an hour. This will help to soften it for cutting. Let it cool before cutting, as there will be hot steam inside.

Cut in half and and clean out seeds and gooey parts. Wash the seeds in a colander now if you intend to roast them, or the gooey stuff will dry on them and make it much harder to clean them later.

Divide your pumpkin into 8 even sections.

Bake in a 350 oven for 40 minutes. Remove from oven, cool, and separate meat from rind. The rind may peel off or you may need a butter knife to separate it, but make sure you cut right down to the rind to make the pieces as thick as possible.

Carefully slice the pumpkin with a mandolin slicer into 1/4 inch slices. Sometimes this is much easier said than done, but salvage what you can. Make sure you use a new or at least a VERY sharp slicer.

As you slice it, place slices on dehydrator trays. Sprinkle with spices you have pre-mixed.

Place the trays in the dehydrator and set to 140F (60C) for 2 to 3 hours, then 130F (55C) until dry.

NOTE: Best if stored in canning jars or zippered freezer bags with clay desiccants and oxygen absorbers. Keep in a cool, dark place.

May last many years in optimum storage conditions.

Pumpkin Seeds

After you have cleaned out your pumpkin, wash the seeds and remove all the glop until they are fully clean.

Put seeds in a pot of boiling water with a tablespoon of sea salt and boil for 10 minutes.

Remove, and blot dry.

Put in a bowl and mix in some sea salt and a small amount of olive oil, enough to barely coat the seeds.

Place in a flat, even, single layer on top of tinfoil on a cookie sheet.

Bake in a 350 degree oven for 30 minutes, stirring a couple of times to rotate them.

Done when crunchy.

Garlic Squash

4 to 5 cups dehydrated butternut squash chunks

1 large onion, chopped

2 tablespoons olive oil

2 teaspoons thyme

1/2 teaspoon salt

1/2 teaspoon pepper

garlic cloves, peeled

Re-hydrate the squash by soaking it in water overnight in your refrigerator. Drain well before preparing.

Preheat oven to 420.

Put cubed squash into shallow pan (9 x 13), add chopped onion, thyme and mix.

Drizzle olive oil over top. Top with salt and pepper. Stuff garlic cloves around edges, as many as you want.

Bake at 420 for 20 minutes, stir and bake another 20-30 mins. Done when squash is fork tender.

Making Super-Pails

I'm sure most of you have heard about storing bulk items in "super pails." This is a fantastic way to store your food long term, but you have to do it right. You can get an unbelievable amount of dehydrated food in a five gallon bucket, and they are lightweight, stackable, and easy to re-seal when you want to remove some of the food.

What you need for each pail:

One new 5 gallon bucket with lid

One Mylar bag, 6 gallon size

Oxygen absorbers

Desiccant packs

A short 2 x 4 or piece of scrap lumber

A common household clothes iron

Whatever food product you wish to store

When you purchase your 5 gallon bucket and lid, try to get the type of lid that fits tightly but is removable and re-usable. Some types (like for paint) fit very tightly and have a gasket, you need to cut the grooves in the lid to get it off once you install it. Also try to get a light-colored lid to be able to write on and have the writing be visible.

The Mylar bags, desiccants and oxygen absorbers can be purchased on ebay or at some health food stores. Get the thick Mylar bags, and make sure you get 6 gallon and not 5 gallon bags, as you need some of the bag to stick out of the bucket to be able to seal them.

I like to get the clay dessicant packs as they are non-toxic and easily re-used one you "re-activate" them (dry them out again).

They make many different sizes of oxygen absorbers, but the higher cc (cubic centimeter) you get, the fewer you need per pail. So I like to get the 300 cc packs and use 3 per pail; that's plenty.

When you have dehydrated enough of a certain food item and you think you have enough to make a super-pail, here's all you need to do and it's fairly easy:

Put the iron in a safe place and turn it on, about halfway. Have the short piece of scrap lumber nearby and handy. Place the Mylar bag in the bucket, and drop a dessicant pack and oxygen absorber in the bottom of the bag. Add the food product about halfway up the bag. Add another desiccant and oxygen absorber to it, and vibrate or lightly shake the bucket to settle the product somewhat. Make sure the bag is being spread out a little to flatten out against the bottom of the bucket. It will not pack it tightly on the bottom, unless you are doing something fine and heavy such as rice or whole kernel corn. Fill the bucket about 2 inches from the top and no more, as you need room to fit the top of the bag in there at the end. Add a final desiccant and oxygen absorber.

Set the board on the edge of the bucket, and make sure the iron is hot and ready. What you are going to do is fold over the top edge of the bag onto the board, and use the board to help seal the bag with the iron. Essentially the wood board works as an ironing board for this. You only want to seal the top 2 inches so you can re-use or re-seal the bag again someday. This takes a little practice as you don't want the iron too cold or too hot. You don't want to melt the bag and have it stick to the iron, but you want to get it hot enough to melt the bag to itself so it seals.

So try a corner, move the iron slowly but firmly, and go over the same area a few times. Let it cool and test it; see if the bag sticks together well. If it does, do about 3/4 of the top edge and let it cool. Once cool enough to handle, fold it inside the bucket so you only have the unsealed part of the bag sticking out. Push the remaining air out of the bag, and make sure it will fit inside the bucket fully and you can get the lid on when finished. If you're cutting it a little too close for space in the bag, now is a good time to pour a little product out before you are done sealing it up.

When satisfied that you will be able to close it, push the air out and finish sealing the bag. Let it cool, push the bag inside the bucket and snap on the lid.

That's it! If done correctly and stored in a cool, dry place, your food should last MANY years.

Just make sure your food is dried **VERY** well before you put it in the bucket and seal it up. You'd hate to open it in a couple years and find it moldy. I will <u>only</u> store food that is so dry it will shatter if bent, nothing "chewy" or semi-moist like raisins, dates, etc. If there's a tiny bit of moisture then the dessicant packs should absorb it, and the oxygen absorbers should inhibit any insects or other types of organisms from surviving.

Always take a permanent marker and write what you stored in each pail on the lid, and the date that you sealed it. In case this info would wear off, I also write the same information on a slip of paper and place it on top of the mylar bag before I put the lid on. This way I could simply remove the lid to see what was inside without cutting into the Mylar bag and then having to re-seal it again.

Cheat – you can use low priced hand warmers instead of expensive oxygen absorbers. The small hand warmer packages you use for wintertime - the ones you open, shake the bag and put in your pockets or gloves to keep your hands warm.

Simply remove the plastic wrap (but don't shake them), and place in the mylar bags. These you can purchase in economy packs, and are much less expensive than regular oxygen absorbers.

Take Notes and Keep a Diary!!

Do this whether you have a small garden in town or a large garden in the country.

It's important to rotate crops and take note of what grew best and where. It's very important to note when you fertilized and with what kind of fertilizer. Keep notes for both spring and fall plantings, as they can vary a LOT where you live.

Notate when you started your heirloom seeds in your starter trays, when you planted them outside, when and what you harvested and how much.

Once you do this for enough years, and you've figured out when to mulch, what to use, how deep to use it and how often, you will get a system perfected of what works best for your garden. Your notebook will be an invaluable tool and a great reference to keep track of all of these things.

Let's face it, food is getting outrageously expensive and there's no reason to assume the prices wil drop. GMO foods are being used more and more often, and there are people growing these foods that are trying to get laws passed so that they don't have to label these foods as being "Genetically Modified."

Why? If they were good for you they'd be advertising it and raising the prices! I'm sure most of us have seen where you can set a store-bought GMO tomato or another type of vegetable or fruit next to one you've grown in your garden,

and see the store-bought GMO kind rot very quickly while the non-GMO foods last for a long time.
And not only that, the pesticides used on these foods are highly toxic. I grew up in farm country and worked on my grandfather's farm years ago. I saw those cans of chemicals they'd dump in their sprayers, and we were always warned to not get ourselves down wind when they were spraying.

This would be bad enough if it went on our lawns, but this is on our FOOD!

Buy heirloom and non-GMO seeds, grow and dehydrate or can your own food, and you will know what it was, how it was grown, and that it was pesticide free.

Some insects can't be avoided. Some can be killed easily (or at least driven off) with natural methods like hot peppers juiced and mixed with water in a vegetable sprayer, and sprayed on certain foods. Or a light spraying of very diluted Dawn liquid soap is relatively a safe way to kill some garden pests. Some you can dust with food-grade Diatomaceous Earth powder which is good for you, but BAD for bugs.

Some insect pests, like "Squash Bugs" are just a certainty during the summer months, and you need to plant early to harvest your produce before they show up. Once these bugs arrive, they kill your plants and you wait for them to leave in the early fall and then re-plant. Come to accept this as a natural part of life and it won't be too stressful. Some people with tiny gardens will pick through their plants daily and physically squish every squash bug they find and have some luck. I tried this and it was too much for me with all of our plants.

So we plant twice a year and accept it.

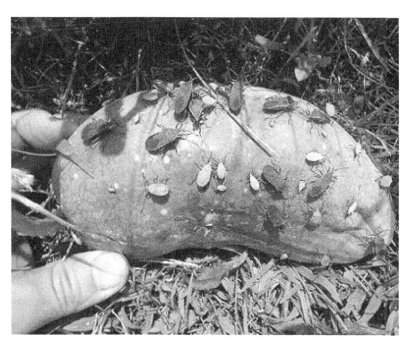

Squash bugs. Half of the bugs fell of this one small melon before I was able to take this photo. They can drive you crazy and kill your plants quickly.

Find a tree nursery in your area and find out what trees grow best where you live. Let them advise you on what time of the year is best for planting, fertilizing and pruning. Some trees are self-pollinating, some need another one like it as a pollinator and some need a slightly different species to cross-pollinate for healthier fruit.

Consider raspberries, blackberries and strawberries, citrus trees if you are far enough south. Consider planting a good asparagus patch with a few different varieties, and if taken care of well, they will give you much asparagus every spring for years and years.

Aphids (enlarged) having a party on our Purple-hull peas. Since we only eat the peas and not the shell like green beans, they don't hurt them.

The more you plant now, the less you have to buy later. Keep pruning and fertilizing notes on the trees, vines and bushes as well.
We don't want to plant trees or bushes in the Shemitah year, but start or plant them the year after Shemitah and by the time the next preparation year comes around, you should have far less to buy. And it will help with the grocery bill as well, of course. And the commandment/requirement for not eating of your new trees will have been fulfilled by the following preparation year.

Leviticus 19:23 *'And when you come into the land, and have planted all kinds of trees for food, then you shall reckon their fruit as uncircumcised. For three years it is as uncircumcised to you, it is not eaten.'*
Leviticus 19:24 *'And in the fourth year all its fruit is set-apart – praises to YHWH.'*
Leviticus 19:25 *'And in the fifth year you eat its fruit, so that it increases its yield to you. I am YHWH your Elohim.'*

Planting Seed and Seed Saving Tips

Buy heirloom seeds that are non-GMO whenever possible. Do some research and talk to other gardeners in your area and see what they grow. Some places have garden clubs; you may consider joining one of those.

Find a place in your home to grow garden plants in starter trays. If you don't have a place, make one. It's easy to fit a 4-foot shelf anywhere and hang a fluorescent grow light over it. It doesn't have to be permanent; take it down when you plant your starts outside. The laundry room is a great place, right over the washer and dryer.

Plus....

Take your starter trays that you have planted your seed in, and when you run the dryer, put your starter trays on top of it, and cover with a towel to hold in the heat. Just lay your towel carefully on top of the tray's cover. The dryer will mimic the heat of the sun shining on the dirt and it makes them germinate and grow more quickly.

Try to purchase starter trays where you can get many separate mini starter trays that are held in one larger base tray. Plant different seeds in the separate little starters, as different plant seeds will grow quicker than others, and the ones that grow fast will quickly need the cover removed from the main tray. And these you simply remove when they get too big and keep them off to the side under the grow light until you plant them outside.

Just make sure you save some of those over-ripe melons, squash and cucumbers to harvest the seeds for your next crop. If you don't have any that are over-ripe, let a couple get that way. Better to leave on the vine and pick the cucumbers when they have gone past green to yellow then possibly orange color. This way the seeds will be good and mature. Plus the softer the fruit is, the easier it is to get the seeds out. Save seeds from <u>everything you grow</u> to use in the next planting season.

Wash them well, dry them and when they are FULLY dry (a couple of weeks later), carefully put them in paper envelopes with detail of what they are and when you grew them written on the envelopes.

Do some research to see how to store them. Some seeds will store at room temperature; some will keep better in the refrigerator. And if you have prepped for a Shemitah, now you need to skip a year before you can plant them, so make sure you store them very well.

What food can we buy during the Shemitah?

We know we can't buy what grows from the land, but we can buy dairy products such as milk, cheese, and butter. We can buy beef, steak, burgers, and all-beef hotdogs. We can buy chicken, poultry, eggs, and clean fish like tuna, salmon, etc.

BUT, buy in the prep year groceries like flour, sugar and such to make hotdog buns, bread, breading for baking fish, and other ingredients that grow or are made from things grown on the land that you need for preparing these meals and meat dishes.

Some may say "Can't we buy bread and buns and just freeze them?"

Well you can, but remember that two weeks after the first of the year (and when the Shemitah begins) comes Passover and the Feast of Unleavened Bread, where we are told to get all the yeast out of our homes. Some people will remove just the yeast itself, while some remove ANY product that contains yeast.

Exodus 12   "*For seven days **no leaven** is to be found in your houses, for if anyone eats what is leavened, that same being shall be cut off from the congregation of Israel.*"

The commandment is that no leaven is to be found in your house, and you surely don't want to make a mistake and eat anything that has leaven in it, either. So we remove <u>all products</u> made with yeast from our home. If you have an alternate freezer that is someplace other than where you live, this may be an option for you. We do not. But we are allowed to buy yeast in the Shemitah when the Feast of Unleavened Bread is completed, so then we can prepare our own bread and buns after that point.

We have to keep in mind what spices that we use as well, as pepper is grown from the land but salt is not. We can buy honey, but we can't buy coffee or tea. The best bet is to go through your kitchen and make a list of what you use the most of and stock up on it before the Shemitah begins. If you don't use all of it during the Shemitah, it will end up saving you money in the long run with the constant price increases in food and groceries.

This may seem like a lot to do and much to go through, but look at it as a fantastic opportunity to obey our Creator! This is part of his covenant and a sign that we are his people. We are blessed to be living in such a time when these things are being unsealed and revealed to us that were hidden for so long! HalleluYAH!

Don't "Glean the Corners of your Fields"

Remember, don't "glean the edges of your fields" so you may have things re-seed and come up by themselves. Those you may eat. You just cannot "harvest" or preserve them. Pick some asparagus, beans, etc. and eat it that day for a meal, or give some to a stranger, or people who need food, and leave the fences open or down for the rabbits and deer to eat some as well.
Don't prune your vines or trees, and obviously we can't sow seed during the Shemitah. Let **ALL** the land rest.

An example of this is what we did with our Rattlesnake beans. I put those tripods up to be a semi-permanent fixture but can still be taken down easily. I will leave them up this fall and winter as we let some of the beans mature and fall that grew and hung inside the chicken wire cages at the bases, that we installed initially to keep rabbits out. So if those come up of their own, they can just grow back up the tripods and we'd have plenty to eat ourselves but most would be given away, if it was a good crop. And in the years when there is no Shemitah the following year, I will take them down and put them in the shed and then put them back up the following spring.

Some scriptural proof:

Leviticus 19:9-10 *'And when you reap the harvest of your land, do not completely reap the corners of your field or gather the gleanings of your harvest. 'And do not glean your vineyard or gather every grape of your vineyard, leave them for the poor and the stranger. I am YHWH your Elohim.'*

And the second witness to that:

Leviticus 23:22 *'And when you reap the harvest of your land do not completely reap the corners of your field when you reap, and do not gather any gleaning from your harvest. Leave them for the poor and for the stranger. I am YHWH your Elohim.' "*

Leviticus 25:4-7 *but in the seventh year the land is to have a Sabbath of rest, a Sabbath to YHWH. Do not sow your field and do not prune your vineyard. 'Do not reap what grows of its own of your harvest, and do not gather the grapes of your unpruned vine, for it is a year of rest for the land. **And the Sabbath of the land shall be to you for food,** for you and your servant, and for your female servant and your hired servant, and for the stranger who sojourns with you, and for your livestock and the beasts that are in your land. **All its crops are for food.***

And in regards to the Shemitah, with a Jubilee year following that:

2 Kings 19:29 *'And this is the sign for you: **This year you eat what grows of itself, and in the second year what springs from that,** and in the third year sow and reap and plant vineyards and eat their fruit.'*

And Isaiah repeated this as a second witness:

Isaiah 37:30 *"And this shall be the sign for you: **This year you eat such as grows of itself, and the second year what springs from that,** and in the third year sow and reap, plant vineyards, and eat the fruit of them."*

So, don't glean the corners of your fields in the preparation year (or during the Shemitah if a Jubilee year follows). Leave some left over to re-seed itself for you, for the animals of the fields, and the strangers to eat as well.

Let's not forget that during the Shemitah -

The Release of Debts

Deuteronomy 15:1-15 *"At the end of every seven years you make a release of debts. "And this is the word of the release: Every creditor is to release what he has loaned to his neighbour, he does not require it of his neighbour or his brother, because it is called the release of YHWH. "Of a stranger you could require it, but your hand is to release whatever is owed by your brother. "Only, there should be no poor among you. For YHWH does greatly bless you in the land which YHWH your Elohim is giving you to possess as an inheritance, only if you diligently obey the voice of YHWH your Elohim, to guard to do all these commands which I am commanding you today. "For YHWH your Elohim shall bless you as He promised you. And you shall lend to many nations, but you shall not borrow. And you shall rule over many nations, but they do not rule over you. "When there is a poor man with you, one of your brothers, within any of the gates in your land which YHWH your Elohim is giving you, do not harden your heart nor shut your hand from your poor brother, for you shall certainly open your hand to him and certainly lend him enough for his need, whatever he needs. "Be on guard lest there be a thought of wickedness in your heart, saying, 'The seventh year, the year of release, is near,' and your eye is evil against your poor brother and you give him naught. And he shall cry out to YHWH against you, and it shall be a sin in you. "You shall certainly give to him, and your heart should not be grieved when you give to him,*

because for this reason YHWH your Elohim does bless you in all your works and in all to which you put your hand.
"Because the poor one does not cease from the land. Therefore I am commanding you, saying, 'You shall certainly open your hand to your brother, to your poor and to your needy one, in your land.' "When your brother is sold to you, a Heḇrew man or a Heḇrew woman, and shall serve you six years, then let him go free from you in the seventh year.
"And when you send him away free from you, let him not go away empty-handed. "You shall richly supply him from your flock, and from your threshing-floor, and from your winepress. With that which YHWH has blessed you with, give to him. "And you shall remember that you were a slave in the land of Mitsrayim, and YHWH your Elohim redeemed you. Therefore I am commanding you this word today."

As you can see this only applies to those in YHWH's covenant, known as Israel. This is just on a personal level, brother to brother, etc. Money lent to those out of covenant is not forgiven; neither are any debts they had incurred from those out of covenant.

This is also prophetic of the Messiah, as the Messiah was given only for those in covenant, as was the covenant given to Abraham and his descendants. Those who wish to have the Messiah forgive their debts (sin), they need to be in covenant and part of the family known as Israel.

The Reading of the Torah During Sukkot

Many years ago and long before printing presses and books, Torah scrolls had to be hand-written. They were very valuable, and not many people had the compilation of the many scrolls required to make up all five books of the Torah that we so conveniently have today in our bibles.

YHWH made it a requirement to have the Torah read every seven years during Sukkot, when all of Israel was gathered together. Imagine being surrounded by huge crowds of people, all eager to hear the word of YHWH.

Deuteronomy 31:10-13 *And Mosheh commanded them, saying, "At the end of seven years, at the appointed time, the year of release, at the Festival of Booths, when all Israel comes to appear before YHWH your Elohim in the place which He chooses, read this Torah before all Israel in their hearing. "Assemble the people, the men and the women and the little ones, and your sojourner who is within your gates, so that they hear, and so that they learn to fear YHWH your Elohim and guard to do all the Words of this Torah. "And their children, who have not known it, should hear and learn to fear YHWH your Elohim as long as you live in the land you are passing over the Jorden to possess."*

Sukkot, also known as "The Feast of Tabernacles," "The Feast of In-Gathering" or "The Festival of Booths" is a fall moed or appointed feast time set by the Creator beginning on the fifteenth day of the seventh biblical month. Sukkot lasts for one week, followed the next day by "Shemini Atzeret." For this week we dwell in a tent or sukkah which is a temporary dwelling, remembering how Israel camped in the wilderness for forty years, in their tents or temporary dwelling places.

Leviticus 23:33-35, 39-43 *And YHWH spoke to Mosheh, saying, "Speak to the children of Israel, saying, 'On the fifteenth day of this seventh month is the Festival of Booths for seven days to YHWH. 'On the first day is a set-apart gathering, you do no servile work. 'On the fifteenth day of the seventh month, when you gather in the fruit of the land, observe the festival of YHWH for seven days. On the first day is a rest, and on the eighth day a rest. 'And you shall take for yourselves on the first day the fruit of good trees, branches of palm trees, twigs of leafy trees, and willows of the stream, and shall rejoice before YHWH your Elohim for seven days. 'And you shall observe it as a festival to YHWH for seven days in the year – a law forever in your generations. Observe it in the seventh month. 'Dwell in booths for seven days; all who are native Israelites dwell in booths, so that your generations know that I made the children of Israel dwell in booths when I brought them out of the land of Mitsrayim. I am YHWH your Elohim.' "*

And that's the end of our little Shemitah preparation book.

We hope you enjoyed it, and our wish is that you may have learned something from it and it might help you in the future with your next Shemitah preparation year.

Shalom from our house to yours, and may YHWH bless you in all that you do as you walk the correct path the Mashiach walked as our example, and he said *"the way you know."*

~ Scott & Gina

See my other book "EXIT BABYLON" for further reading into being obedient to YHWH. This is a large book with many chapters on what religion teaches that is not correct.

Available on Amazon and Kindle.

Text from the back cover of "EXIT BABYLON":

There is a new trend in Christian churches today. Many have withdrawn from or are being asked to leave their congregations when they begin to question the doctrines practiced by their churches, realizing that what is being taught from the pulpit does not match the Word of the Creator.
Those seeking truth are now searching the scriptures for themselves, awakening to the troubling fact that what is done today in the churches is a result of truth having been compromised and believers having been deceived, as prophecy warned that even His elect could be in these last days. Many appear to be hearing the call to "come out of her, my people," are leaving the churches behind, and walking away from the confusion known as Babylon.

The Creator is in the process of calling his people out of Babylon. I didn't know what that meant until I started to explore scripture for myself, which led me to the path walked by our Messiah. **He did NOT do** *what Christianity claims. Christians can't see the truth because their thought process is blinded with dogma, doctrine, and traditions of men.*

This book is not "religious." I am not promoting Christianity, Judaism, or ANY type of religion. The **ONLY** *thing I promote is living by the Word of our Creator. I strive to live by and practice what the Messiah taught, which is that very Word and nothing else.*

Most people think the "antichrist" and the "mark of the beast" will be manifested in the future; however, they have been here already for quite some time. Almost EVERYONE right now - on this very day - has already been marked by the beast. The mark has nothing to do with social security numbers, barcodes, computer chips or RFID tags. It is far more simple than that. You may be shocked by just how easily this can be seen and proven by using the Word.

Over forty five topics are discussed in this book, and the facts are confirmed with scripture. Included is a summary of what is going on in Christianity today, and what truth seekers need to be made aware of. The end is near, and we are very likely MUCH further along in the prophetic timeline than most people realize. This written work is a plea for those who are His, having eyes to see and ears to hear, to discern the signs of our times and ***EXIT BABYLON.***

Also from Beit Tefillah Publishing, a new book that is a must-have for the remnant, and those who wish to observe the moedim/feasts of YHWH by the truth of His word and not by the traditions of men;

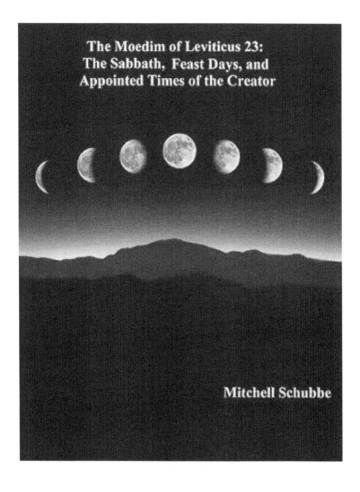

Available on Amazon and Kindle.

Text from the back cover of "The Moedim of Leviticus 23: The Sabbath, Feast Days, and Appointed Times of the Creator":

Deuteronomy 30:8 *"And you shall turn back and obey the voice of* יהוה *and do all His commands which I command you today."*

Many are hearing the call to exit Babylon and to turn back in obedience to the Word. Unfortunately, in a rush to find truth, many are pulled into a ditch filled with the doctrines of men, simply exchanging one set of traditions for another. In "The Moedim of Leviticus 23: The Sabbath, Feast Days, and Appointed Times of the Creator", each chag, moed, feast and festival is carefully explored using only the scriptures, and explained in a way that enables you to drop your traditions TODAY and begin to walk in the Way. The Sabbath, Passover, Unleavened Bread, First Fruits, Pentecost, the Feast of Trumpets, Yom Kippur and the Feast of Tabernacles, as well as the shmita and jubilee years are discussed and explained using each verse in the old and new testaments which speaks directly of those appointed times. The traditions of men are shattered and the pure doctrine of the Word is shown, highlighting the role of the Messiah in each of these days.

Also included is a special bonus chapter on a modern Hebrew wedding, outlining each of the prophecies about Messiah returning for his spotless bride.

Isaiah 56:7 *My house shall be called a house of prayer for all people.*

Made in the USA
Monee, IL
15 November 2022

17822470R00075